♥ ♥ THE MAGICAL WORLD OF ♥ ♥
AMY LEE

Dedicated to all my Cute Recruits!

Big thanks to Lilly Ladjevardi for making this book happen.

Scholastic Children's Books
Euston House, 24 Eversholt Street,
London NW1 1DB, UK

A division of Scholastic Ltd
London ~ New York ~ Toronto ~ Sydney ~ Auckland
Mexico City ~ New Delhi ~ Hong Kong

First published in the UK by Scholastic Ltd, 2016

ISBN 978 1407 17100 5

Printed and bound in Italy

2 4 6 8 10 9 7 5 3 1

♥ ♥ THE MAGICAL WORLD OF ♥ ♥
AMY LEE

📖 SCHOLASTIC

Contents

Here are a few tips and ideas for getting the most out of my book.

This symbol means it's your turn to get creative! So wherever you see it, draw or write in the space provided.

You all know how much I love seeing drawings and crafts from you cuties. So wherever you see this symbol, you can ask your parent or guardian to share a picture of that drawing or craft project with me! Here are the ways they can share pictures with me:

- Twitter: @AmyLee_thirty3
- Instagram: @amylee_33
- Facebook: amylee33.minecraft
- PopJam: AmyLee33

Staying safe online:

Always get permission from your parent or guardian before sharing pictures online. Never post any personal information online, such as your real name, address, phone number, email address or the name of your school. And beware of posting pictures that could clearly identify you.

Land of Love Quiz

Are you a super-fan? How well do you really know the adventures I've had in the Land of Love? Take this quiz to find out if you're a top Cute Recruit or if you need to brush up on your knowledge. You get one point for every question you get right. See page 106 for the answers.

1 Who was my very first dog?

2 What's my favourite colour?

3 What did Mittens turn into when he made a wish in the Wishing Well?

4 Which dog saved me from the Witch when she tried to cook me in the Gingerbread Tea House?

5 Which dog is the puppy of Boomer and Lola?

6 What did I find living on the moon when I looked through the telescope?

7 What was the name of the first film I watched in the movie theatre on Halloween?

8 What are my pet squids called?

9 What is the name of the evil wizard who stole the sword from Sir Warrick and Sir Garroway?

10 What is the name of the friendly creeper I made in the Secret Laboratory?

11 What is my bow and arrow called?

12 What is there a picture of outside the Witch's lair?

13 Name one of the four cookie flavours in the Cookie Cafe.

14 What is the name of my Prince Charming?

15 What did the fairies use to decorate the Land of Love at Halloween?

What does your score mean?

0-5 Don't worry, cutie. You've got more to learn, but you'll have lots of fun exploring the Land of Love!

6-10 Good work, that's a great score. You have obviously joined me for lots of adventures already!

11-15 Wow! I just can't even. You must be my number one fan! Well done on your amazing score.

Amy's Friends

Stampy

Likes: cake

Dislikes: googlies

Most often found: in his Lovely World

Catchphrase: "Hello, this is Stampy!"

My favourite thing about him: I love how creative Stampy is with his Lovely World. And he always makes me laugh!

One thing you might not know about him: he is not technically a cat – he is a Nimbat!

Sqaishey Quack

Likes: building and playing games

Dislikes: meanie beanies

Most often found: in a pond or trying to fly

Catchphrase: "Don't be a meanie beanie!"

My favourite thing about her: I love Sqaishey's singing

One thing you might not know about her: she likes to organize things!

iBallisticSquid

Likes: bows and arrows

Dislikes: drowning

Most often found: screaming his head off in a mini game!

Catchphrase: "Hello everybody!"

My favourite thing about him: Squid always makes me laugh uncontrollably!

One thing you might not know about him: when he first started making Minecraft videos his skin was an old professor. It was Stampy who suggested it would be a good idea to use the squid skin since his name was iBallisticSquid!

StacyPlays

Likes: buckets of milk, and dogs

Dislikes: crabs called Crusty

Most often found: in a Mesa biome or the Candy Isle

Catchphrase: "I died"

My favourite thing about her: I love that Stacy secretly really loves Crusty!

One thing you might not know about her: she met an untimely end after an incident with a penguin in an episode of Hexxit.

Amy's Friends

Netty Plays

Likes: buckets of water. It's one of the first things she makes – her ultimate weapon!

Dislikes: baby zombies and cave spiders

Most often found: playing Speed UHC

Catchphrase: "Dun dun duuuuun!"

My favourite thing about her: Netty's laugh always makes me giggle!

One thing you might not know about her: she has never been to an underwater temple.

Mousie Mouse

Likes: magic, dragons and adventures

Dislikes: the colour red and mean monsters

Most often found: on an adventure!

Catchphrase: "Stay S'Wonderful!"

My favourite thing about her:
Mousie is very smart and always has the right answers!

One thing you might not know about her: in Mousie's world, Jane the dog is named after Jane from Tarzan!

Ash Dubh

Likes: sponges, 'cos they look like cheese

Dislikes: sponges, 'cos they're not cheese. Skelebobs and gravel

Most often found: in the Hive playing Death Run

Catchphrase: "Stay cheesy", "wow", "get out of town" and "I wasn't ready!"

My favourite thing about him: when Ash says "Woooooooooooow!"

One thing you might not know about him: his first ever Minecraft skin was based around Ash from Pokemon due to an old school friend calling him Ketchupy for his whole school life.

Salems Lady

Likes: lapis lazuli and her squishy slimes

Dislikes: creepers and not having a lapis sword

Most often found: collecting more animals in her survival world

Catchphrase: "Ore-some!"

My favourite thing about her: Salem is fearless and always looks out for me!

One thing you might not know about her: she can never remember how to make a Minecraft cake. Shhhh, don't tell Stampy!

Meet the Family!

Lexi

What makes her special: first dog found. Oldest dog and mother of the pack.

Loves: pink

Personality: very girly but also mature. She likes to look after the other dogs.

Max

What makes him special: second dog found. Father of the pack and the first dog named by viewers. His full name is Max Power!

Loves: adventures with Amy!

Personality: very brave and protective.

Luna

What makes her special: first puppy born in the Land of Love.

Loves: flowers and nature – she always joins me on nature adventures.

Personality: kind and mellow. She's a hippy dog!

Mars

What makes him special: bravest dog (he rescued me from the Witch).

Loves: protecting his family.

Personality: charming and heroic.

Sailor

What makes him special: Sailor is very adventurous.

Loves: water and swimming – he loves anything to do with water.

Personality: usually brave, but he was scared by the Halloween movie!

Dogs:

My dogs are my best friends in the Land of Love – they really are family to me! I have so much fun with them and they're all so different. Take a look at their family tree.

Lola

What makes her special: Lola is super intelligent.

Loves: books

Personality: Lola is the smart dog and always knows what to do.

Destiny

What makes her special: Destiny was born in episode 100 when I became a princess!

Loves: the stars and anything to do with space. She loves to hang out at the observatory.

Personality: very calm and sometimes gets lost in her daydreams!

Boomer

What makes him special: he was a wild dog who joined the pack. I found him with a bunch of creepers and tamed him.

Loves: computers and science! He also has a soft spot for the beasties.

Personality: Boomer doesn't like to battle with the beasties unless he is protecting his family.

Romeo

What makes him special: he's the only puppy of Lola and Boomer.

Loves: horses and hanging out at the stables.

Personality: Romeo is a boisterous dog who thinks he is a cowboy!

Meet the Family!

Cats:

My three kitty cats are so cute and playful. I love curling up on my bed with them – although they don't always leave much room for me or the dogs!

Saturn

What makes him special: Saturn was my first ever cat.

Loves: his adopted little brother Comet, going out with me and fish!

Personality: protective of the other cats.

Comet

What makes him special: I adopted Comet after I found him as a baby kitten wandering alone in the jungle.

Loves: his adopted big brother Saturn.

Personality: Comet can be a little jealous of new kitties.

Star

What makes her special: Star is my first female cat.

Loves: salmon

Personality: a little shy, but once she found her confidence she fitted in with the other cats.

Iron Golems:

Bert and Bertha are tough soldiers who protect my house from beasties. They are married to each other.

Bert

Bert is strong and focused – he can't be distracted when he's on a mission!

Loves: his number one hobby – block staring! He loves Bertha very much too, almost as much as the block of the day.

Bertha

Bertha has beautiful ruby red eyes, but she's not good at spotting me over her big iron nose!

Loves: protecting me and my family, and she loves her Bert.

Snow Golems:

My three cheeky snow golems are always having fun and getting up to no good. Mittens is the naughtiest of the gang!

Mittens

Very mischievous! Mittens just loves to pull pranks and drive me crazy, but he has a heart of gold. He can be very brave and saved me from the Witch at Christmas time.

Blizzard

Unlike Mittens, Blizzard is usually a very good golem. But sometimes he just can't resist Mittens' crazy schemes.

Mr Frost

Just like Blizzard, Mr Frost is usually well behaved. That is until Mittens comes up with something mischievous...

Love: all my golems love music, dancing and crazy adventures.

Personalities: mischievous, fun-loving and messy, but very caring and lovable.

Horses:

I adore horses! One of my favourite things to do in the Land of Love is take one of the ponies out for a ride in the show jumping arena.

Journey

Journey was my first horse. He loves to go on nice long rides out into the forest.

Tinkerbell

The second horse I got. My dog Romeo shares a wonderful bond with Tinkerbell.

Lily

My foal born to Journey and Tinkerbell.

Moonbeam

Strong and mysterious. Moonbeam is Mittens' favourite horse.

Gabriel

My first donkey. Gabriel is incredibly fast!

Grandfather Oak

My tree spirit and a really spiffing old chap!

Loves: telling stories, watching over my house.

Personality: wise, kind, old.

Peace Pig and Peace Chicken

These two cuties live in my Garden of Peace and Love.

Love: flowers, love and peace.

Personalities: calm, peaceful, happy, loving.

Pick a Pet!

I love having so many doggies! They all have different personalities, so whatever mood I'm in, I've always got the perfect companion. Take this fun quiz to find out which dog would be the perfect pet for you.

Do you love the outdoors?

Yes. I hate being cooped up inside.

No. I prefer curling up on the sofa.

Not really, I prefer comedies.

Do you like scary movies?

Yes – the scarier the better!

Do you always come top of the class at school?

Yes. I work hard and always do my homework on time.

No. I find it hard to concentrate on schoolwork.

Would you rather go for a hike through a meadow or go swimming in the sea?

Meadow – I love walking and picking flowers.

LUNA

You're a flower child, just like Luna! You're relaxed and kind, and you love being outside.

Sea – I love swimming and being at the beach.

SAILOR

Like Sailor, you love the water! You're adventurous and love being at the seaside.

Would you rather read a book or play on your computer?

Books – I love discovering new worlds and stories.

LOLA

Just like Lola you love losing yourself in a book. You're clever and trustworthy – people can always rely on you.

Computer – I love new technology and being creative.

BOOMER

You love knowing how things work, just like Boomer. You're a good friend and a whizz at computers.

If you see someone in trouble do you jump straight into action to help them?

Yes, I'm always alert and ready to be brave.

MARS

Like Mars, you're an action hero! You will always lend a hand and everyone wants to be your friend.

Not really, I'm usually daydreaming so wouldn't notice.

DESTINY

You've got your head in the clouds, just like Destiny. You're thoughtful, calm and a bit of a daydreamer!

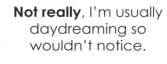

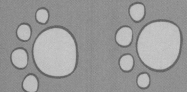

25

Collar Quiz

How well do you know my doggy family? Each one has a different-coloured collar – can you match the right dog with the right collar colour? I've done the first one for you to get you started.

Lola

Destiny

Romeo

Lexi

Mars

Sailor

Boomer

Max

Luna

Doggy Logic

The dogs decided to have a race. Can you work out who came in which position using the clues below? I've filled in a couple of answers to give you a head start.

- ➤ Lexi is behind Max, Luna and Mars.
- ➤ Sailor is behind Mars and in front of Lola, Boomer and Romeo.
- ➤ Mars is in front of Lexi, Sailor and Boomer.
- ➤ Lola is behind Boomer, Destiny and Luna.
- ➤ Max is behind Luna and in front of Lola, Romeo and Destiny.
- ➤ Boomer is in front of Romeo and Lexi.
- ➤ Romeo is behind Lola, Max and Sailor.
- ➤ Luna is in front of Mars, Lola and Sailor.
- ➤ Destiny is behind Luna and in front of Boomer, Romeo and Sailor.
- ➤ Lola is behind Lexi and Mars.
- ➤ Mars is in front of Max and Romeo.
- ➤ Boomer is behind Max, Luna and Destiny.

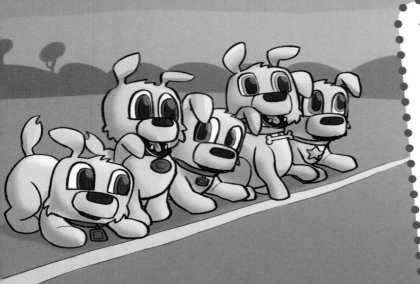

1st ....
2nd ....
3rd ....
4th Destiny ....
5th ....
6th ....
7th ....
8th ....
9th Romeo ....

DISAPPEARING DOGS

Iiiiit's feeding time!

"Hello, my little lovelies!" I float into the room, looking at all nine adorable doggie faces. "Are you hungry?"

The dogs look up at me, panting eagerly.

"Would you like a baked potato?"

They stare at the piping hot potato. Their tails stop wagging.

"No? How about some fishies?" I hold out a smelly, slippery fish. The dogs whimper and look down at the floor.

"No? No fishies?"

I can't help giggling. "Oh, I love to tease you so! I brought steaks for each of you!"

Seeing the fat cuts of meat, the dogs' eyes light up and their tails start wagging again.

When every dog has eaten their fill, I step back and look them all over.

Hmmm.

"Who wants to go with me on today's adventure? I was thinking we could go to the garden and build a mud bath for Peace Pig! Wouldn't that be fun? Let's see ... Lexi? Sailor? I haven't been on an adventure with Mars for a while now. How about it, Mars? Would you

like to go for an adventure?"

Mars twitches, and his ears perk up.

"Loves it. Come on, then, follow me!"

I make my way into the hall, down the stairs and out the front door, with Mars happily trotting alongside.

It's a beautiful morning in the Land of Love: the sun is shining, the birds are singing and there are clear skies all around – all except for a lone dark cloud approaching fast!

"Look, Mars!" I say. "That cloud looks almost purple. Do you think it might rain?"

The cloud passes over the house, casting a dark shadow. Suddenly there is a blinding flash.

BOOM!

The thunder is so loud I can feel my whole body shake. Mars, terrified, streaks off into the distance. Moments later, all the other dogs burst from the house, scattering in all directions.

"Stop!" I shout. "Darlings, it's only a little storm!"

But even as I say the words, I wonder: is there more to that cloud than meets the eye?

So much for building a mud bath today. I need to find my doggies!

TO BE CONTINUED...

Help me find my dogs! Can you spot eight of them before you reach page 62?

Cat Craft

I love my kitty cats just as much as I love my doggies. Here's a super-fun and easy art project so you can create your own cat friends. This is especially fun to do around Halloween time since black cats are kind of spooky!

You will need:

- **Toilet paper roll**
- **Black paper**
- **Sticky tape or glue**
- **Black paint** (optional)
- **Scissors**
- **Felt-tip pens**

Instructions:

1 Wrap the toilet roll with black paper and secure in place with sticky tape or glue. Alternatively you can paint the toilet roll black.

2 Draw a circle a little bigger than the open end of the toilet paper roll onto some extra black paper. Add ears, legs and feet as shown in the picture.

3 Draw a second circle the same way, and add a tail, legs and feet.

Top Tip

You can make the face even more realistic by cutting the whiskers, eyes and nose from coloured card and sticking them on.

4

Ask an adult to help you carefully cut out the two shapes. Then draw in the eyes, whiskers and nose onto the face.

5

Put a generous amount of glue on the edge of the roll. Carefully place the head on the glue and let it dry. Repeat on the back. Make sure the feet on the back are level with the feet on the front.

6

That's it! Your little cat is finished. What will you call your new friend?

Top Tip

Try trimming the length of the toilet roll to make a whole family of kitties!

Spot the Difference

Can you find 10 differences between these two pictures of Bert and Bertha on their wedding day?

The Art of Amy Lee

You will need:

- a piece of plain paper
- a pencil
- an eraser
- a black pen
- coloured pens or pencils

1

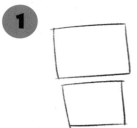

Using a pencil, draw two boxes one above the other. The bottom box should be slightly smaller than the top one.

2

Now add long balloon shapes (as shown) to make the arms and legs.

3

Draw an oval shape around the top box.

Top Tip Don't worry if you make a mistake, just rub it out and start again!

4

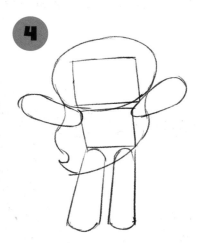

To turn the oval into hair, add wavy lines going down and meeting in a point.

5

Add four semi-circles: two for eyes, one for a mouth and one on top of the hair.

6

Now we're adding in the fine details. I've drawn arrows to show where to add each detail.

7

When you're happy with your drawing, go over the lines with your black pen to clean it up and round the edges. Wait for it to dry and then rub out the pencil marks with an eraser.

8

Finally colour in your picture with your colouring pens or pencils. Hooray, you're all finished!

Amy-ism Dictionary

Everyone knows I say "loves it!" all the time, but here are a few of my other top catchphrases. Do you have any of your own?

Silly gooseberry

The magic is real!

You're a good egg

Everyone needs a tree for a friend

Beasties

Lovely jubbly love love petals

Cute

Storytelling with Grandfather Oak

Grandfather Oak is the best storyteller I know. He is very old and wise so he has a lifetime of stories. Not everyone can hear his stories though – only people with the best imaginations.

Can you write one of his stories here? Maybe it's about a pirate who's discovered some long-lost treasure, or a ballerina about to perform for the first time, or maybe a girl who wakes up one day and discovers she can talk to animals! It can be about anything you like. If you want, you can use the ideas on the next page for inspiration.

Characters:

- a pirate
- a clown
- a princess
- a horse
- an orphan
- a ballerina

Plot ideas:

- someone runs away from home
- a magical object is discovered
- someone discovers a secret door
- there is a shipwreck
- someone is kidnapped by a witch
- someone gets a huge surprise

Settings:

- a haunted house
- the beach
- boarding school
- a misty forest
- a ship at sea
- the zoo

Adjectives:

- friendly
- strange
- mysterious
- sparkly
- pretty
- gigantic

Plan your story here!

One day in a little town called Skegness
their tired a princess called maisy.
One saterday Maisy went to the beach then
she found a pearl

Write your story here

Top Tip

If your story is too long to fit, just continue on another piece of paper. You could always stick it into the book afterwards to keep it all together.

Amazing Inventions

I love using my imagination to come up with new ideas and inventions. I created a secret laboratory so I have somewhere to go and do my creating. My favourite ever invention was my knight vision goggles! The ghost of an old knight was haunting my house, but I couldn't see him, so I invented these special goggles to help me see ghosts. Problem solved!

I love being creative, but even more than that, I love hearing your amazing ideas. You guys are always so imaginative and you come up with the coolest suggestions. So why not create your own incredible invention here?

Fill in the details below and then draw a picture of your invention opposite. Be as creative as you can – the possibilities are endless!

What is your invention called?

....

....

What does it do?

....

....

Are you remembering to look for my dogs? You should have found five by now!

Random Acts of Kindness

My world isn't called the Land of Love for nothing! I want to spread love all around the world. One of the most amazing ways to do this is with random acts of kindness towards people and animals.

My top 10 random acts of kindness are:

1 Talk to someone at school who is new or looks lonely.

2 Write a note to someone you care about – share a positive thought about them, fold it up and place it somewhere they will be surprised to discover it.

3 Donate your old clothes and toys to charity.

4 Help older people – you could offer your seat on a train or help them with their luggage.

5 Feed birds in the winter.

6 If you see a bug trapped inside, carefully put it outdoors.

7 Say thank you to your parents for everything they do.

9 Hug a tree. I always say, everyone needs a tree for a friend!

8 Help around the house without being asked to do so.

10 Love yourself too! Don't beat yourself up when you do something wrong – think of it as a learning opportunity.

It's important to be grateful for what you have and help people less fortunate than you. You can spread love and kindness just by smiling and sharing positive thoughts!

Can you come up with some of your own ideas here?
Fill in the details below and spread the love!

Wishing Well

I believe that dreams can come true! That's why I built a wishing well in the Land of Love. What would you wish for if you had a magic wishing well?

46

i wish i CoulD beCoMe A DoG AgAin!

47

Lovely Jubbly Necklace

I love nature and being out in the Garden of Peace and Love. I especially love filling my world with colourful lovely jubbly love love petals! And here's a fun way to have flowers with you all the time – a beautiful pressed-flower necklace of your very own.

You will need:

- garden or wild flowers
- kitchen roll
- A4 paper
- five large microwaveable plates
- a microwave
- a wide roll of clear sticky tape
- scissors
- tweezers
- a hole punch
- a reel of ribbon

48

1 Select a few pretty flowers that will lie flat easily, such as daisies and pansies. Don't pick anything that is wider than your roll of sticky tape and remember to get permission from the owner of the garden.

2 Clean and dry the flowers with kitchen roll.

3 Tear a scrap piece of A4 paper in half. Place a piece of kitchen roll on top of one half of the paper.

4 Carefully arrange your flowers on top of the kitchen roll. Try to flatten the flowers as this will help them press better.

5 Lay a second piece of kitchen roll gently over the flowers, making sure they remain flat, then cover with the remaining spare paper.

6 Carefully lift the flowers and paper onto a large microwaveable plate, then stack 3–4 more microwaveable plates on top.

Top Tip To start with, press one variety of flower at a time until you are used to your microwave and the settings.

7 Place in the microwave for 30 seconds. Then ask an adult to carefully take the plates, paper and kitchen roll off the flowers. Your flowers should be dry, stiff and very flat. If they are not, return them to the microwave for another 30 seconds.

Top Tip If you don't have a microwave, put your flowers and paper in a magazine and pile books on top. Leave them for 2–4 weeks, changing the kitchen roll regularly as it will collect moisture.

8 Collect all your pressed and dried flowers. Unpeel a long piece of sticky tape and lay it on a table, sticky side up. Using tweezers, gently arrange your flowers face up on the sticky tape, making sure there is space between each flower or group of flowers.

9 Cut another length of sticky tape, at least as long as your first piece. Carefully line up the edge and stick it on top of the flowers, smoothing the two pieces of sticky tape together gently with your hands.

10 Carefully cut around each flower or group of flowers, leaving enough tape at the top for a hole. Then use a hole punch to create the hole. If your flower shape is too small, ask an adult to make the hole using scissors.

11 Cut a length of ribbon long enough to go around your neck and thread your flowers onto it. Tie at the back and wear your beautiful lovely jubbly necklace!

Perfect Paw Prints

My garden has been visited by some wild creatures in the night.
Can you match up each paw print with the animal who left it?
See page 107 for the answers.

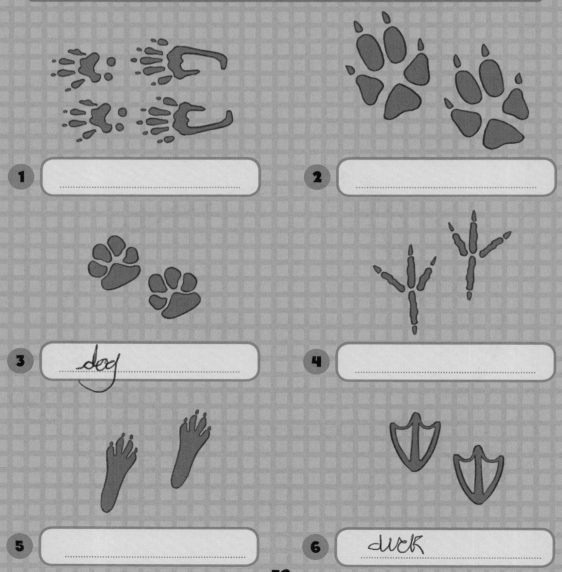

1 ....

2 ....

3 ...... dog ....

4 ....

5 ....

6 ...... duck ....

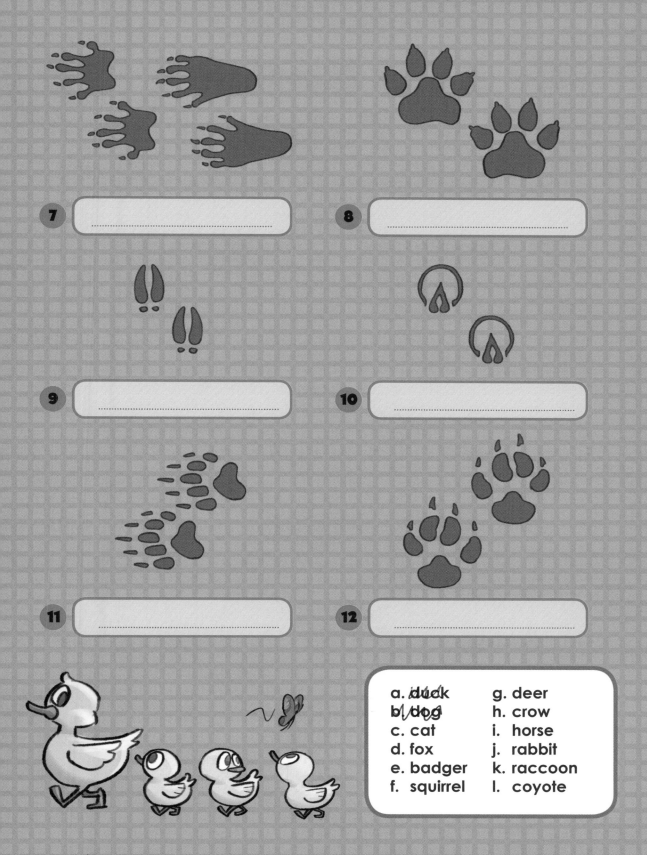

7 ....

8 ....

9 ....

10 ....

11 ....

12 ....

a. ~~duck~~
b. ~~dog~~
c. cat
d. fox
e. badger
f. squirrel
g. deer
h. crow
i. horse
j. rabbit
k. raccoon
l. coyote

I Do Believe in Fairies!

The fairies in the Land of Love just love creating surprises for me. Sometimes they put up decorations in the night or leave out presents. Other times they write me secret messages in fairy code.

Can you use the code below to help me work out what the message opposite says?

1 = a	p = h	h = n	% = u
x = b	* = i	@ = o	8 = v
# = c	4 = j	6 = p	c = w
2 = d	l = k	d = q	€ = x
t = e	¥ = l	£ = r	9 = y
$ = f	5 = m	7 = s	m = z
3 = g		z = t	

Why not make up your own code and use it to write top-secret notes to your friends?

2t1£ 159,
dear amy

Ct p18t #£t1zt2 1 z£t17%£t
p%hz $@£ 9@% 1h2 9@%£
$£*th27 z@ th4@9. #1h 9@%
$*h2 t8t£9zp*h3 ct p18t
p*22th? Z%£h zpt 613t z@
$*h2 @%z!

p18t $%h!

¥@z7 @$ ¥@8t,
Zpt ¥1h2 @$ ¥@8t $1*£*t7

€€€

Treasure Hunt

How fun! The fairies have created a treasure hunt for us. Can you help me find 10 gold coins that they have hidden around the Fairy Lagoon?

Pine Cone Bird Feeder

This is a really fun and easy craft project, plus a brilliant way to make sure birds have enough to eat in the winter. It's so satisfying to look out the window and watch the birds eating from your homemade bird feeder.

You will need:

- string
- a large pine cone
- peanut butter
- mixing bowl
- wild bird seed

Instructions:

Tie the string to the top of the pine cone.

1

2

Cover the pine cone with peanut butter. Make sure you get the peanut butter into all the cracks and crevices until the pine cone is completely covered. If you warm the peanut butter up a bit, this is even easier.

3

Pour the wild bird seed into the mixing bowl. Then roll the peanut butter-covered pine cone in the bird seed. Roll it back and forth to completely cover it and press the bird seed in with your fingers to help it stick.

4

Now just take your awesome bird feeder outside and find the perfect place to hang it. Tree branches are ideal. It's nice to hang it outside a window so you can watch the birds feeding. Make sure it's high enough off the ground that cats and dogs won't disturb the birds who come to feed.

Dive In and Colour!

THE WITCH ATTACKS!

It's been a long afternoon. I stand back and count the dogs my Cute Recruits and I have managed to round up.

"Darlings, stay still. Luna, Lexi, Max, Sailor, Boomer, Lola, Romeo, Destiny – that only makes eight."

I count again – just to be sure. But my feeling of uneasiness is growing.

"...six, seven and eight. Where's Mars? Has anyone seen Mars?"

Oh, no. We've searched every corner of the Land of Love, but Mars is still missing! Where could he have gone?

Suddenly, I hear barking in the distance. It's coming from the school!

I burst inside the school's entrance doors.

I don't see Mars. I do see Mittens, though, standing in the corner and holding a big grey book.

"Mittens, dear, this is no time for stories. Have you seen Mars?"

Mittens holds the book out to me.

I sigh in frustration. "Not now, Mittens; we'll read stories later. We need to find Mars!"

Suddenly I hear a barking sound ... now coming from just outside. Mars? I spin around and—

Uh-oh. The entrance doors are blocked with spider's webs. We're trapped!

Then, out of the corner of my eye, I see a flash of purple.
It's the Witch.

All at once, I understand the Witch's cunning plan. By scaring away the dogs with thunder, she made sure that I would be outside all afternoon, giving her time to kidnap Mars and lure me into this trap.

Well, it's not over yet! I can still stop the Witch and save Mars. I reach for my bow, Katniss, but the Witch is too fast. She has her wand out, and before I even touch Katniss—

I stare out, frozen. No matter how hard I try, I am unable to move.

The Witch has cast a spell on me!

But why? What does she want?

Uh-oh. I should have known: she's going to take over this book! I can't stop h—

TO BE CONTINUED...

AH HA HA HA HA HA! Amy can't move. This book is now mine, all mine!

My Greatest Moments

AHAHAHA! I'm in charge now, and you're all under my spell. Amy's always telling you that I'm evil and she never gives me credit for my amazing ideas. Well I'm going to put the story straight and tell you about my most brilliant plans.

5 ## Kidnapping Mittens

Oh, this was a good one! I kidnapped that horrid snow golem Mittens and trapped him in a cage in my secret lair. My spiders were guarding him, but Amy and Luna fought us and managed to get away with Mittens. Ugh!

4 ## Poisoned Apple

On Valentine's Day, I put on a disguise and tricked Amy into eating a poisoned apple. While she was passed out I kidnapped her and locked her up. It was working perfectly, but then Prince Oliver rode in and rescued her. He ruined everything!

3 Tea with Amy

Heehee, I tricked Amy into thinking I wanted to be her friend. I lured her into the Gingerbread Tea House and pushed her into the boiling water of the oven! I thought I'd killed her for sure, but then her bothersome dog Mars pulled her out in the nick of time. So annoying!

2 Bringing Dracula to Life

When Amy and Sailor went to the movies one Halloween, I snuck in and cast a spell to bring the vampire from the movie to life! Clever, wasn't it? The vampire and I then broke into Amy's room and I trapped her with webs so the vampire could bite her. But that pesky creeper, Ralph, came back and chased us away. Very tiresome.

1 Santa Disguise

This was one of my greatest ideas! On Christmas Eve I disguised myself as Santa Claus and trapped the real Santa in spider's webs. I stole his magic boots so he couldn't deliver presents to all the children. But that troublemaker Mittens threw snowballs at me and chased me away. Foiled again!

Hubble Bubble

What is your evil potion called?

....

....

What ingredients are in it?

....

....

What does it do?

....

....

Draw a picture here to show what your potion does:

Spider's Web Maze

Haha! It's my book now! So no more of that cute and cuddly nonsense. Let's see you try and escape my fiendish spider's web maze. Can you sneak through without my spiders catching you? The answer is on page 108.

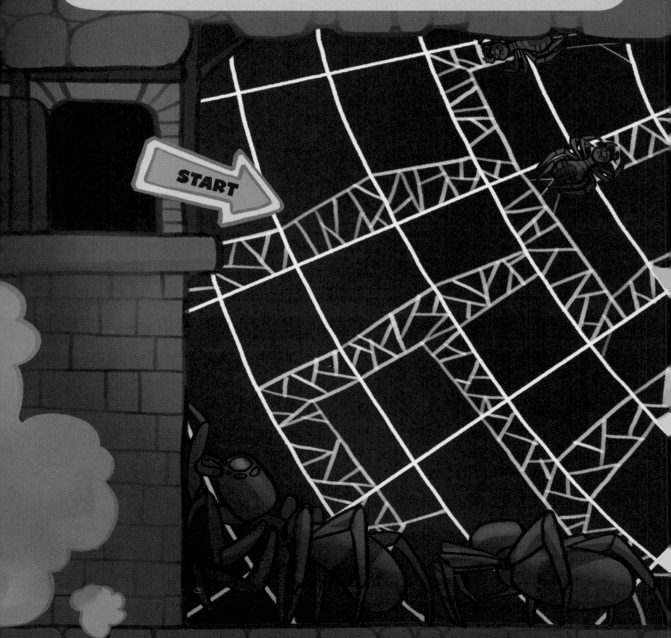

Loathsome Lair

Now that I'm in charge of the Land of Love, I think it's time I had a new house to live in. No more hiding up the mountains – I'm going to have a huge lair right in the middle of Amy's world. I just need to find some minions to build it for me...

MITTENS MAKES MISCHIEF

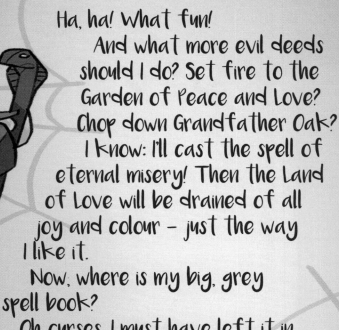

Ha, ha! What fun!
And what more evil deeds should I do? Set fire to the Garden of Peace and Love? Chop down Grandfather Oak?
I know: I'll cast the spell of eternal misery! Then the Land of Love will be drained of all joy and colour – just the way I like it.
Now, where is my big, grey spell book?
Oh curses, I must have left it in the school

Here we are. Now, where's my lovely book of spells?
Oh, there it is – that silly snow golem is holding it. Hang on, are his lips moving? That's odd: can snow golems even speak?
Oh, no, he's casting a spell! And wait – is Amy moving? She's free! And she's got her bow and sh–

POOF!

The Witch disappears in a cloud of smoke. My arrow went right through it! I lower Katniss, relieved that she's gone ... for now. And I finally have the book back!

"Oh, Mittens, you funny bundle of loveliness – you cast a spell and released me! I'm so sorry for brushing you off before, I didn't realize you were trying to give me the Witch's spell book." I give him a big hug. A slight blush pinks up his icy cheeks.

Awesomeness! All my friends are safe and Mittens is the hero of the day. Loves it!

"Mittens, I think it's finally time to build the Peace Pig a mud bath, don't you?"

Mittens smiles a mischievous smile and points to the door. I open the door and—

GASP!

"Oh my goodness. There's a massive evil building right in the middle of everything! Did that nasty witch put the Cute Recruits under her spell and make them build her a home?"

Mittens nods and holds out the Witch's spell book to me.

"That's a great idea, Mittens. I'll just cast a spell to make it go away. Here, you hold this book, while I take the spell book. Mittens – hang on, where are you going? ARE YOU TRYING TO TAKE OVER THIS BOOK, TOO—?"

TO BE CONTINUED...

Can you unscramble these words to reveal 10 things that I love?

1 MISUC

MUSIC

2 CANDING

3 WONS

4 AVENDUTERS

5 MAY

6 TARPIES

7 MOBMOENA

8 BASLLSNWO

9 CHASMTISR

10 GOSD

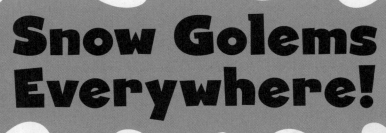

Snow Golems Everywhere!

woohoo! i've reopened the portal into the snow golem world and sneaked out to have another party. can you spot me in the crowd? i've dressed up extra smart for the party, wearing a black bow tie.

My Greatest Moments

Hooray! i am everyone's favourite mischievous snow golem. i'm always having adventures and getting up to no good! Here are my top 5 greatest moments in the Land of Love.

5 making Myself a cute Recruit

The other snow golems and i snuck out of the house and added ourselves to the cute Recruit patch. Amy found us in the dance studio because we love to dance!

4 Saving Bert and Bertha's Wedding

When Bert and Bertha got married, they didn't have any rings. But i found some and saved the day at the last minute! i was the hero.

78

3 misbehaving in school

On my first day in school, i was quite naughty! i snuck off to ride a pony instead of coming straight to class, threw snowballs at the blackboard, jumped over the hedge during recess and went for a boat ride, made the wrong potions in science and threw more snowballs in the cafeteria! i did say sorry in Detention though!

2 my house party

i invited hundreds of snow golem friends over for a house party! The loud music woke Amy up at night, and she discovered that snow golems were coming through a portal. She went through the portal into the snow golem world... And turned into a snow golem.

1 Turning into a Dog

i made a magical wish in the wishing well And turned into a Dog! i just wanted to have a fun day out with Amy, outside of the house. And we had so much fun! it was my best day ever.

Spot the Difference

CAN YOU FIND 10 DIFFERENCES BETWEEN THESE TWO PICTURES OF BLIZZARD, MR FROST AND ME GETTING UP TO NO GOOD?

Playful Pranks

1 This Coin trick is HILARIOUS! Secretly colour in the edge of a coin with a pencil. Then bet someone they can't roll the coin from their forehead down to their chin without the coin leaving their face. When they do this they are left with a dark line down their face. Teehee!

2 Ooh, another fun prank with a coin. Glue a coin to the ground and wait for people to try and pick it up — it's so funny!

3 Try putting sugar in the salt shaker and salt in the sugar bowl. Just don't forget you've done it and accidentally sprinkle sugar all over your chips!

4 This prank will really gross people out! Put a raisin inside a napkin and pretend to have caught a fly. Then eat the raisin in front of everyone!

5 This one is great to play on your brother or sister. Get some plastic bugs and put them inside a cereal box. Then watch them scream as they pour bugs into their breakfast bowl!

ENOUGH MISCHIEF!

"**M**ittens, you're so naughty!" I say, trying to catch my breath. "I think we've had enough of your mischievous pranks; this is Mummy's book."

Chasing Mittens is hard work. He's so speedy! Good thing he leaves a snowy trail; otherwise I'd never have found him and got back this book!

Mittens looks down at the ground, and I can't quite tell if he's ashamed – or just disappointed for having been caught. I think he's disappointed; he never seems to regret his naughtiness!

"I know, darling, you were having lots of fun," I say. "And I'm sure all the Cute Recruits have really enjoyed your games. But I'm not finished with the book yet. So you run along now, Mittens. Maybe you can go play some games with Mr Frost or Blizzard? They must have missed you!"

Mittens perks up, flashes a smile and slides away, back towards the house.

"There you go. Love you muchly!"

Phew! Now everything's finally back to normal and we can get on with building Peace Pig's mud bath. This book is not leaving my sight ever again!

THE END

Cute Crossword

Can you complete this fun Land of Love-themed crossword?

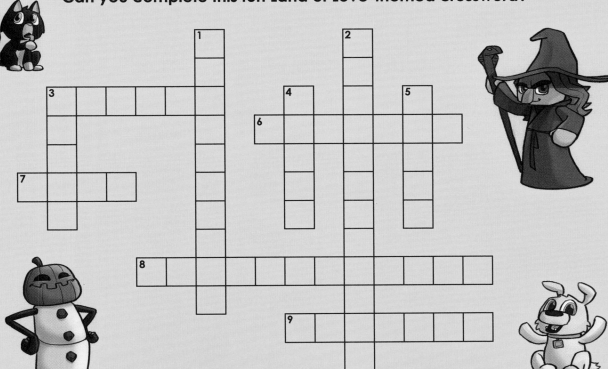

Across

3. My first cat and the sixth planet from the sun (6)

6. My number one catchphrase! (5, 2)

7. My favourite colour (4)

8. What do I call a red rose? (6, 6)

9. My favourite mischievous snow golem (7)

Down

1. Where I live and the name of my series (4, 2, 4)

2. What my fans are called (4, 8)

3. Inky and Nugget are both this animal (5)

4. My eighth dog and married to Juliet in Shakespeare's play (5)

5. My worst enemy in the Land of Love (5)

Paper Dolls

Have you ever wanted to bring the characters from the Land of Love to life? Well, now you can with these super-cute creations. Just follow the instructions below to make your very own Land of Love paper dolls.

Instructions:

1 Cut out pages 85 and 87 from the book, or make a colour photocopy if you prefer.

2 Roughly cut out each figure and glue them onto card.

3 When the glue is dry, carefully cut around each figure and fold the stand back where shown.

4 That's it – your paper dolls are finished! Now you can create your own stories and adventures in the Land of Love.

Top Tip

You might need an adult to help you with the cutting out.

Amy

FOLD   FOLD

Mittens

FOLD   FOLD

Stick
this side
to card

The Witch

FOLD   FOLD

Max and Lexi

FOLD   FOLD

FOLD   FOLD

Stick
this side
to card

What's Your Princess Name?

Have you ever wanted to know what your princess name would be? Use the chart below to work it out! Just combine the date of your birthday (which will be your first name) with the month you were born in (which will be your surname). For example, I was born on 29th July, so my princess name would be Pearl Stardust! Funsies!

DATE

1st	Daisy	17th	Violet
2nd	Crystal	18th	Angel
3rd	Bluebell	19th	Lavender
4th	Emerald	20th	Primrose
5th	Rose	21st	Aria
6th	Iris	22nd	Petal
7th	Ruby	23rd	Coral
8th	Jasmine	24th	Hope
9th	Amber	25th	Ivy
10th	Poppy	26th	Sapphire
11th	Luna	27th	Destiny
12th	Topaz	28th	Peaches
13th	Lily	29th	Pearl
14th	Holly	30th	Scarlet
15th	Strawberry	31st	Willow
16th	Melody		

MONTH

January	Sparkle
February	Blossom
March	Diamond
April	Dazzle
May	Twinkle
June	Rainbow
July	Stardust
August	Berry
September	Glitter
October	Shimmer
November	de Fleur
December	Sunshine

My princess name is  topaz dimond

Design a Tiara

My dreams came true the day I was made a real princess! The King and Prince Oliver crowned me with my very own beautiful tiara.

If you were a prince or a princess, what would you want your tiara or crown to look like? Would it sparkle with hundreds of red rubies, or have your initials carved in gold? Design your own tiara or crown in the space opposite.

Draw your tiara here

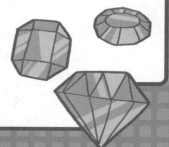

Underground Maze

Oh no! I was digging underground and hit lava!
Can you help me take the right path through
the maze to escape without perishing?

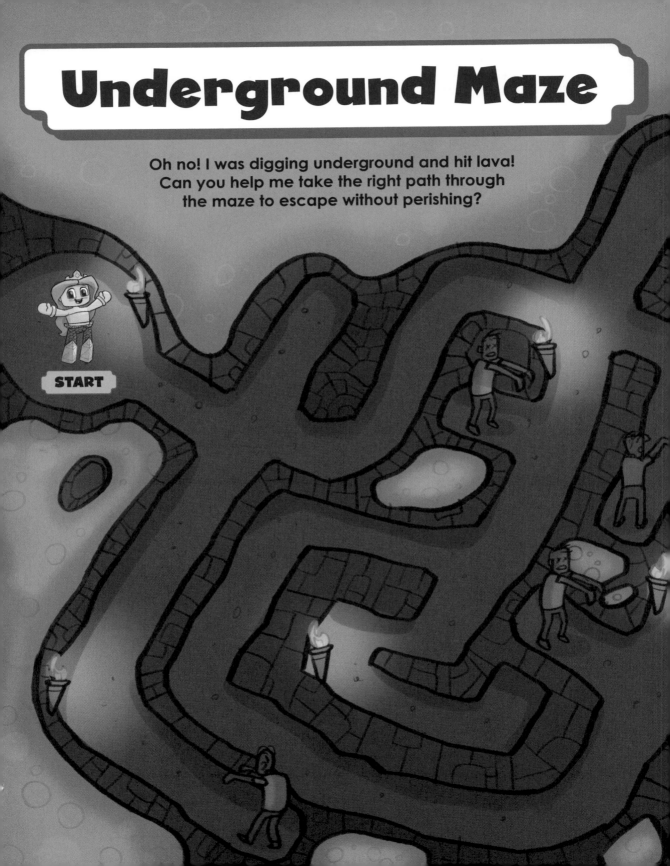

FINISH

Cute Colouring

Fun Facts

1 Before becoming a mermaid, my skin was actually a wolf!

2 I named the red rose a "lovely jubbly love love petal" in one of Stampy's Lovely World videos.

3 My favourite piece of armour is my diamond boots.

4 If I could add any new items to Minecraft it would be more golems and animals like tigers, monkeys and penguins. Plus silver ore to make jewellery!

5 Snow golems are my favourite mob!

6 My favourite build is my Gingerbread Tea House.

7 I really wish the Witch would like me!

8 Nearly all my animals and creatures were named by viewers.

9 My favourite weapon is my bow, Katniss!

10 If I were stranded on a Minecraft desert island and could only take four items, I would take my dog, Mars, flint and steel, my bow, Katniss, and melon seeds. What would you take?

Fun with Friends

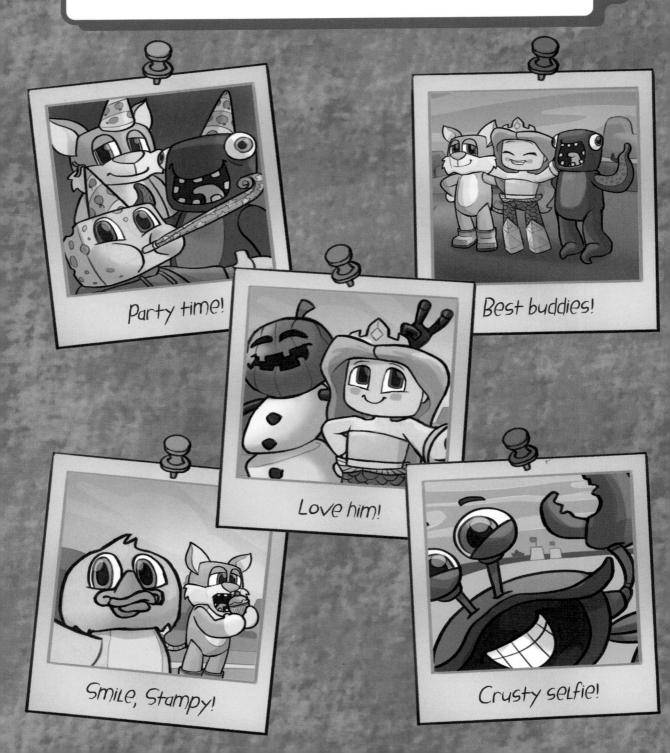

Party time!

Best buddies!

Love him!

Smile, Stampy!

Crusty selfie!

Mittens mischief!

Cuties!

Hanging with the boys!

My favourite girls!

Swimming with Stacy!

Nom nom nom!

Dreamcatcher

I thought it would be fun to make a dreamcatcher to keep bad dreams away and make sure you guys have lovely dreams every night. Plus it will look super cute in your room!

You will need:

- **paper plate**
- **scissors**
- **hole punch**
- **paint** (optional)
- **yarn or string, any colour**
- **craft feathers**
- **craft beads**
- **stickers or colouring pens** (optional)

Instructions:

1

Cut the centre of the paper plate out, leaving a rim of about 5cm all around the edge.

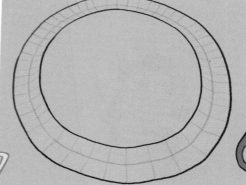

2 Use the hole punch to punch holes around the rim of the paper plate, about 2cm apart.

3 If you want, paint the paper plate circle any colour you like.

4 Next, cut a long strand of yarn or string around 1.5–2m long. Tie one end of the yarn to any of the holes on the rim of the paper plate.

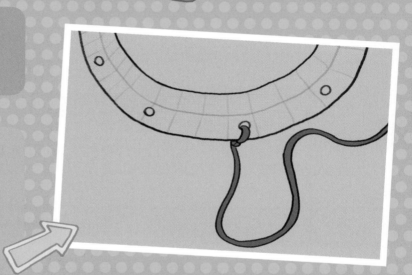

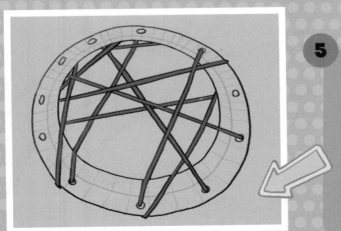

5 Weave the yarn up, over and around the paper plate from one hole to the next in a criss-cross pattern. You can make the pattern any way you like, just make sure you loop through each of the punched holes.

6 You can also add beads to the middle of the dreamcatcher. To do this, simply slip a few beads onto the yarn before continuing through the next hole. The beads will appear in the middle of the dreamcatcher.

7 Once all of the holes are threaded with the yarn, tie the end of the yarn to the last hole with a knot.

8 Now, use the hole punch to punch three more holes at the bottom of the paper plate circle.

9 Cut three more pieces of yarn, about 10–15cm long each, and tie them to the three punched holes at the bottom of the dreamcatcher.

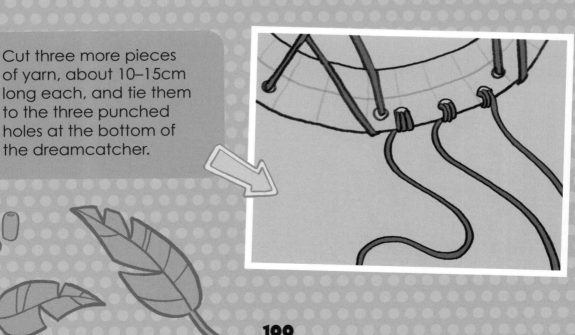

10

Thread a few beads onto each of the three strands and then tie a feather to the end of each. This will look super cute and stop the beads slipping off.

11

If you want, use stickers and colouring pens to decorate the edges of the dreamcatcher.

12

Lastly, cut a piece of yarn the length you need to hang it on the wall. Punch one more hole at the top of your dreamcatcher and tie the yarn to it.

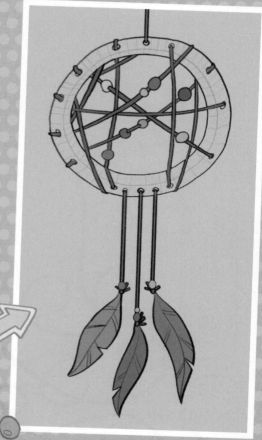

13

Hang your dreamcatcher above your bed and enjoy sweet dreams!

Dreamcatchers have been a traditional part of Native American culture for generations. They have the power to protect you from bad dreams! The idea is that the string web traps the bad dreams, whilst good dreams glide down the feathers onto the sleeping person. The hoop symbolizes strength and unity.

In a Tangle

Bert and Bertha found Mars in a tangle of leads outside the school, where the Witch had left him. We each grab a lead, but which of us is connected to Mars?

Together Again!

Hooray! Finally all my puppies are back home safe and sound. Thank you for helping me find them. Did you spot them all?

You're a Cute Recruit!

Congratulations!

Well done for completing all the challenges. You're now officially a Cute Recruit, so fill in the certificate opposite with your name and today's date. If you want you can photocopy it first so you can stick it up somewhere for everyone to see! I hope you've had fun solving puzzles and being super creative. Don't forget, guys... Amy Lee loves you!

Cute Recruit Certificate

This is to certify that

.... *sophie* ....

has been awarded a Cute Recruit certificate
for being super awesome!

Congratulations!

Date: 15 . 1 . 17

Signed: Amy Lee xx

ANSWERS

Pages 14–15
Land of Love Quiz

1. Lexi
2. Pink
3. A dog
4. Mars
5. Romeo
6. Space Aliens
7. Fright Night
8. Nugget and Inky
9. Malice
10. Ralph
11. Katniss
12. A mushroom
13. Luvsit S'more Cookie!,
    Mermaid Munchie!, Flour Power,
    CoCo Delight Cookie!
14. Prince Oliver
15. Spider's webs

Page 26
Collar Quiz

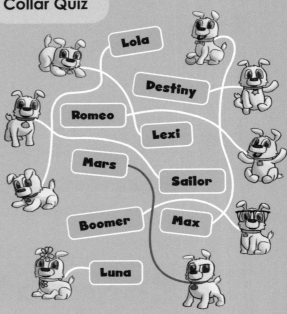

Page 27
Doggy Logic

1st Luna
2nd Mars
3rd Max
4th Destiny
5th Sailor
6th Boomer
7th Lexi
8th Lola
9th Romeo

Pages 32–33
Spot the Difference

Pages 52–53
Perfect Paw Prints

1. f (squirrel)
2. d (fox)
3. c (cat)
4. h (crow)
5. j (rabbit)
6. a (duck)
7. k (raccoon)
8. b (dog)
9. g (deer)
10. i (horse)
11. e (badger)
12. l (coyote)

Pages 54–55
I Do Believe in Fairies!

Dear Amy,

We have created a treasure hunt for you and your friends to enjoy. Can you find everything we have hidden? Turn the page to find out!

Have fun!

Lots of love,
The Land of Love Fairies

xxx

Pages 56–57
Treasure Hunt

ANSWERS

Pages 68–69
Spider's Web Maze

Page 76–77
Snow Golems Everywhere!

Pages 74–75
Mittens Takes Over!

1. MUSIC
2. DANCING
3. SNOW
4. ADVENTURES
5. AMY
6. PARTIES
7. MOONBEAM
8. SNOWBALLS
9. CHRISTMAS
10. DOGS

Page 80
Spot the Difference

Page 83
Cute Crossword

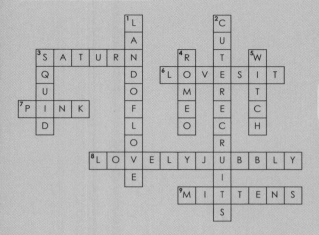

Pages 92–93
Underground Maze

Page 102
In a Tangle

It's Bert! Bert has Mars on his lead.

Pages 30–62
Find the Dogs

Page 31: Max
Page 33: Lexi
Page 34: Sailor
Page 37: Lola
Page 42: Boomer
Page 45: Destiny
Page 46: Romeo
Page 48: Luna